THE ORCHESTRAL
SNARE DRUMMER

By Anthony J. Cirone

ANTHONY J. CIRONE
Percussionist – San Francisco Symphony
Associate Professor of Music – San Jose State University

A Non-Rudimental Approach to the Teaching of Snare Drum

A Companion Book to
The Orchestral Mallet Player
and
The Orchestral Timpanist

I DEDICATE THIS BOOK TO MY MOTHER, MARTHA CIRONE,
who got me started in drumming and kept me going with her unend-
ing love and patience.

FOREWORD

Although the subtitle of this snare drum method is "A Non-rudimental Approach to Beginning Snare Drum," rudiments do play a major role in the technical training of the student. The important difference is that the actual performing is approached in a manner that is more conducive to orchestral, symphonic band, studio and jazz training. The rudiments will only apply (with exception) to the actual development of technique and do not necessarily have to be carried over in the development of reading.

The rudiments are in two categories:
1. Rudiments that are written for in the orchestral literature.
2. Rudiments that are not written for in the orchestral literature.

The students are asked to play in many different meters - other than $\frac{2}{4}$ $\frac{4}{4}$ $\frac{3}{4}$ so that the later transition to modern time signatures will not be difficult.

In order not to clutter up the pages with excessive comments, I have left the obvious explanations such as rests, bar lines, time signatures, etc., up to the instructor.

All reading exercises contain a second line which would normally be played by a second player on bass drum. A third player could also play with crash cymbals. It is not intended for the student to tap his foot on these notes. The top line could also be played by triangle, tambourine, castanets (without flams) to form a percussion section. Refer to *Orchestral Techniques of the Standard Percussion Instruments* for correct technique on bass drum, cymbals, tambourine, triangle, castanets. (Available from Cirone Publications, P.O. Box 612, Menlo Park, Cal. 94025.)

The Orchestral Snare Drummer is a companion book to *The Orchestral Mallet Player* and *The Orchestral Timpanist*. Each of these books functions as a beginning method for its instrument and together these methods cover the three basic areas of total percussion: snare drum, keyboard percussion and timpani.

The etudes included in the three books were written with two objectives in mind: (1) to provide original solos for the various instruments which may be performed independently and (2) when played in conjunction, the three books provide pieces which can be used for ensemble performance, beginning with the most elementary of percussion set-ups.

THE TRADITIONAL GRIP
The technique for grasping the snare drum sticks is as follows:

Right Hand - The thumb and forefinger grasp the stick about 1/3 from the butt end. The stick should rest at the first knuckle joint of the forefinger. The remaining fingers should close around the stick. The back of the wrist should face up. The wrist should not be in a vertical position. The hand should be relaxed in its most comfortable position. The wrist provides the up and down motion; the fingers underneath the stick should move with the stick and not remain stationary. The motion should come from the wrist and not the arm.

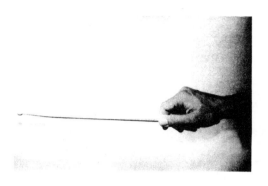

Left Hand - The stick should rest in the fleshy area at the base of the thumb about 1/3 from the butt end. The forefinger and middle finger relax over the stick; the ring finger and pinkie relax under the stick. The pressure should only be exerted by the thumb. The two fingers on top of the stick only act as a guide and in advanced techniques provide a rapid single stroke rebound. The two fingers underneath the stick should not be touching the stick when it hits the drum. The stick should be free to produce a big sound. When the fingers are touching the stick, the sound tends to become more staccato. The wrist of the left hand should be in a vertical position. The wrist motion of the left hand is that of a rotating motion. The arm should not be used for the up and down motion. Although the arms are not used for the basic stroke, they do move in conjunction with the wrists when performing.

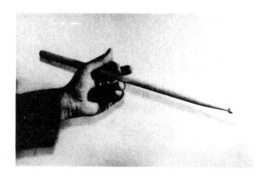

or

THE MATCHED GRIP - students utilizing this grip will have both hands follow the instructions for the Right Hand as listed above.

Considerations for choosing a grip:
1. If a student is extremely right-handed, the traditional grip may prove to be more satisfactory.
2. Ambidextrous students may find the matched grip more to their advantage.
3. As experience is showing in the professional field, there is also an advantage to learning both grips.
4. Extremely left-handed students may also try reversing the traditional grip.

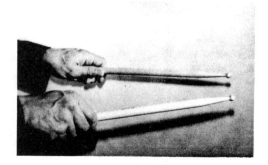

These considerations particularly apply to the amount of pressure needed at the fulcrum of the grip for the loud roll. If a student has a weak left hand, the strong thumb pressure of the left hand traditional grip may prove to be more advantageous than the forefinger and thumb of the matched grip.

PROPER EXECUTION

Once the student has been shown the correct method of grasping the snare drum sticks, a great deal of importance should now be placed on the proper execution of the sticks on the drum or pad.

The bouncing of the sticks can be properly taught by comparing it to the natural bouncing of a ball. As a ball strikes a surface it rebounds upwards and then falls again to the surface. The natural force of gravity pulls the ball towards the surface. When releasing the snare drum stick a similar action must be obtained. The wrist motion should never interfere with the bouncing action, it should only follow the natural bounce of the sticks.

Now as a ball keeps bouncing, each successive bounce would become smaller and smaller. With the snare drum technique, the wrists should be used to provide just enough force to allow each bounce to remain equal. The wrist motion should not be used to force the stick into the drum.

Just as a ball always bounces off a surface, the stick should always bounce off the pad or drum. Never allow the wrist to restrict the sticks from producing this motion.

To develop complete control in mastering this technique, a student should begin by executing very slow strokes and then gradually increase the speed. As the first few strokes are the slowest, they would also be the highest strokes and the student should use a very large wrist stroke and even some arm motion. As the strokes become faster the wrist and arm motion become less. The prime consideration is always to follow through with the stroke just as in the natural bouncing action of a ball.

My thanks to JOE SINAI for his collaboration on the bouncing ball idea.

Single Strokes

As a general rule, all single strokes are alternated, only in technical exercises do we vary the sticking. As with all rules, there are exceptions, however, we will not be concerned with them at this point. Start with your strongest hand, if you are right-handed that would be your right hand and vice versa.

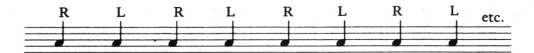

All the beats of the measure must be counted - even the rests.

Bass drum and cymbal should play the bottom line. The correct muffling technique should be used to stop the sound; muffle only the rests that coincide with the snare drum rests.

Double Strokes

For our purpose in training the orchestral snare drummer, double strokes are only used in developing technique and the roll. When we read rhythms, we only use single strokes.

A very basic exercise which should be practiced every day is commonly called the m a m a - d a d a. It is simply a double-stroke exercise which forms the development of the roll.

slow to fast

At first, practice slowly - always trying to make each stroke sound the same. As you feel confident, begin to increase your speed, but only to a point that you can control every stroke.

Combination of single and double strokes

single paradiddle

double paradiddle

triple paradiddle

The previous rudiments are in the category which are not written for in the orchestral literature.

These exercises should be practiced daily.

Single Stroke Exercises

1

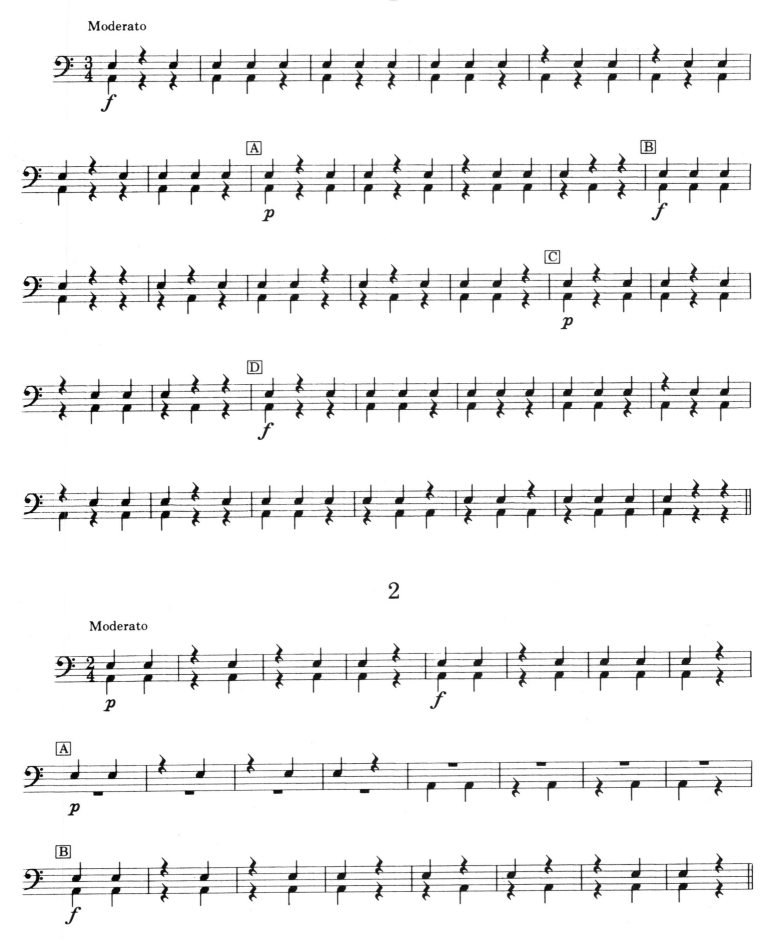

The Closed Roll

All snare drum rolls with the exception of the rudimental drum-corps roll are CLOSED ROLLS. The louder the roll becomes, the more open it becomes, but never to the point of only two bounces on each stick.

A CLOSED ROLL should be taught first and as the student progresses, the OPEN ROLL can then be introduced (for technique practice).

etc.   Slow to fast

The bounce stroke — This stroke is performed with one motion of the wrist and always consists of more than two bounces. The idea here is the same as with the double bounce exercise, each hand should produce the same sound. At first, the student will produce a very uneven sound, but as long as he can sustain the sound without measuring the roll (i.e., 5-stroke roll, 7-stroke roll, etc.), the desired effect will soon be produced. I firmly believe the students should not be taught the measured rolls at first, it gives them a completely incorrect attitude of what a roll should sound like. A roll is a sustained, continuous sound that does not have a certain number of beats. A roll begins at one point and ends at another. A roll should always be tied into a single note (for our purpose) and the note should be heard as a normal quarter note.

This roll begins on 1 and ends on 2; the tempo will determine the amount of strokes needed.

Although both ways must be mastered, a right handed student should begin the rolls with his right hand and vice-versa.

Rolls and Single Strokes

Eighth Notes

Eighth note patterns are counted with the use of AN. Only count the notes that are played. Of course, all the counts that fall on the main beats must be counted whether they are rests or notes.

If the student has good coordination, he may tap his foot on the main beats, (quarter note pulse) otherwise the foot should not be used.

Eighth Note Studies

6

DRUM SECTION SOLOS

Top line may be played by:
    Snare Drum — Triangle — Tambourine — Castanets

Bottom line may be played by:
    Bass Drum — Crash Cymbals
Tempo may vary from Andante to Allegro

9

10

MORE DRUM SECTION SOLOS

In the next five pieces the time signatures of $\frac{2}{8}$ $\frac{3}{8}$ $\frac{4}{8}$ $\frac{5}{8}$ and $\frac{6}{8}$ will be counted in eighth notes.

That is each eighth note will be given one count. Ex. $\frac{3}{8}$ $\overset{1\ 2\ 3}{\text{♫}}$

13

15

16

17

The Flam

The name given to the sound of two sticks striking the drum very close together is a FLAM. The sticks should never strike the drum at the same time, but very close together. In order to consistently produce this sound, one hand should be higher than the other; then releasing both sticks, one stick should strike the drum slightly before the other. The FLAM STROKE can be produced by the right hand starting higher than the left or viceversa.

Although both ways must be mastered, I suggest a right-handed person perform most flams with his right hand and a left-handed person with his left hand high. The FLAM must be played with one motion of both hands not two separate motions.

For consistency and control, it is suggested that whenever there are two or more FLAMS in a row, they should all be produced with the same FLAM. Therefore, do not alternate FLAMS.

After a right-hand FLAM, a left stroke should be used and viceversa.

Two excellent rudiments to practice for the development of the FLAM are:

It is suggested these stickings be used when reading music, but it is not absolutely necessary.

Flam and Single Strokes

When the triangle and tambourine are also playing the top line, they should ignore the FLAMS. Only the snare drum plays the FLAMS.

18

19

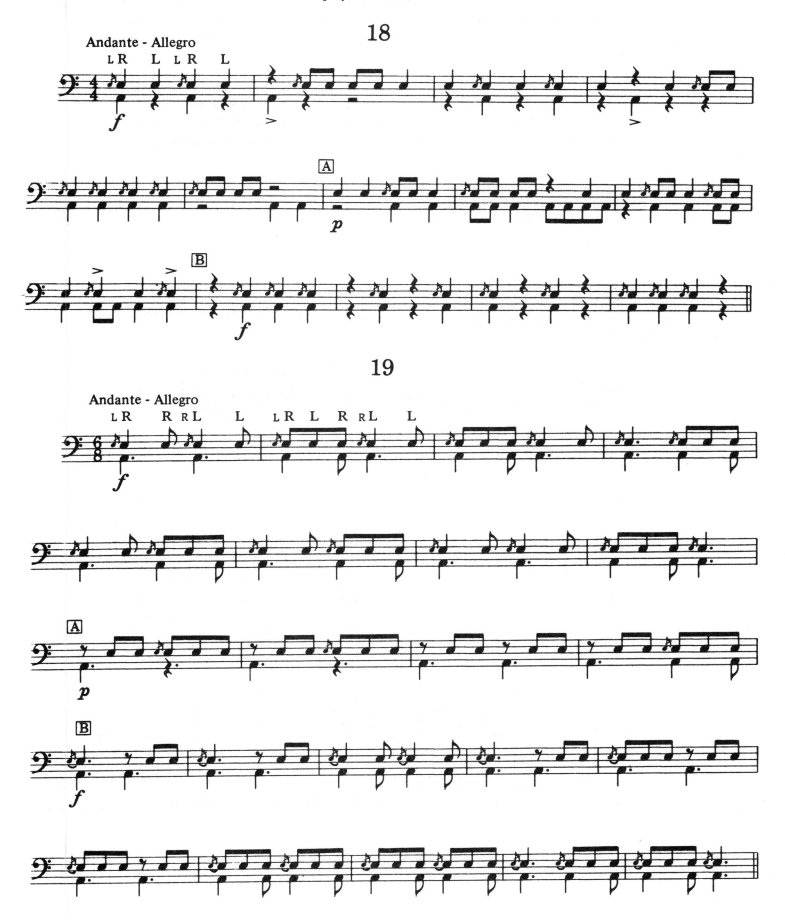

Flams, Rolls, and Single Strokes

20

21

The Drag

A DRAG (sometimes called a ruff) is notated with two grace notes. Since the rudiments are played closed in the orchestral literature, this figure is not executed as it may appear. Instead of playing two strokes for the grace notes, they should be played as a closed bounce stroke very close to the main note.

The same rules apply to the DRAGS as with the FLAMS. If there are two or more DRAGS in a row, play them with the same hand so as to produce the same sound. Do not alternate the drags.

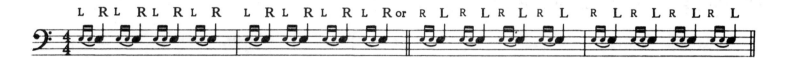

One hand should start higher than the other as with the FLAM technique. The accent should always be on the main note and not the grace notes.

The following rudiments are not written for in the orchestral literature, however, they are useful in the development of the DRAG.

The DRAG may be played open (two strokes) for military music.

Drags, Rolls, and Single Strokes

22

Drum Section Studies
using flams, drags, rolls and single strokes.

24

25

The 5 Stroke Roll

A 5 STROKE ROLL is a rudiment that composers write for in the orchestral literature. For our purpose in this book and also for most literature, the 5 STROKE ROLL should always be played CLOSED.

The four notes preceding the quarter note are always written as grace notes. They should be played as close to the quarter note as possible. Therefore, as the tempo becomes slower or faster the speed of the 5 STROKE ROLL remains the same.

The 5 STROKE ROLL may be started with either the right or left hand as indicated above. This rudiment begins and ends with the same hand. If one was to play the figure above with the sticking that is notated, an open 5 STROKE ROLL would result. Since this rudiment must be played closed, instead of playing two right-hand strokes and two left-hand strokes, the right and left hand should each play a closed bounce — similar to the roll stroke. When playing a closed 5 STROKE ROLL only three motions are needed: a bounce on the right hand, a bounce on the left hand and a single quarter note at the end (right hand). Remember the strokes must be played very close together so one sound results and the accent must always be at the end.

Sixteenth Notes

I feel it is very important for the percussion student to be able to say verbally what he is playing rhythmically. It is not so important what he says as long as it fits rhythmically. One method of counting sixteenth notes is to use the syllables 1-e-an-da. The foot keeps the pulse on the numbers, therefore, keeping a quarter note beat.

The next two forms of sixteenth note rhythms are:

The counting is taken from the 1-e-an-da. Only count the notes that are played.
The main beats of all rhythms are counted whether they are notes or rests.

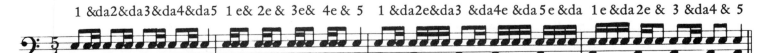

DRUM SECTION STUDIES
using sixteenth notes, flams, drags and rolls.

29

30

Rolls on the Bass Drum should be played with two small Bass Drum beaters or two Timpani sticks. The entire Cymbal part should be played on a Suspended Cymbal with two yarn mallets.

31

When playing sixteenth notes in $\frac{2}{8}\frac{3}{8}\frac{4}{8}\frac{5}{8}\frac{6}{8}$ etc., the sixteenth notes should be counted as eighth notes. Ex.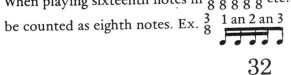

32

33

34

Triplets

A **TRIPLET** is one of many super-imposed rhythms. When three notes are played
in the same time as two notes of the same value, we call this a **TRIPLET**.

Ex.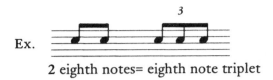

2 eighth notes= eighth note triplet

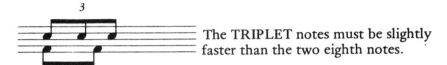 The **TRIPLET** notes must be slightly
faster than the two eighth notes.

For our purpose in this book we will only be concerned with eighth note **TRIPLETS**.

Combinations of Eighth Notes, Sixteenths and Triplets

36

37

Andante - Allegro
1   2 an da 3

38

The 4 Stroke Ruff

This rudiment is composed of three grace notes preceding a given beat. The three grace notes are played as single strokes but so quickly that the sound is as one fat note.

The emphasis should always be on the final note. It can be started on either hand and as with the other grace note rudiments, it should not be alternated.

Prepare to execute this rudiment in the same position as a FLAM, with one hand higher than the other. Then drop both sticks at the same time, allowing each stick to strike the drum twice. Since one hand is lower, it will strike the drum before the other, therefore, the four notes will alternate very quickly.

At first the 4 STROKE RUFF can be played as four single notes, however, the final result should be executed in one motion.

The 7 Stroke Roll

The 7 STROKE ROLL like the 4 STROKE RUFF and 5 STROKE ROLL is written for in the orchestral literature. All the rules that applied to the 5 STROKE ROLL also apply here.

The 7 STROKE ROLL begins with one hand and ends with the other. Be sure to use closed bounce strokes on each hand and the accent must always be at the end.

Changing Meter

In the following exercise, the time signature changes from $\frac{2}{4}$ to $\frac{3}{8}$. I suggest the eighth notes be counted in this manner:

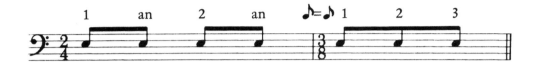

In the $\frac{2}{4}$ measure you can count in the normal manner, however, in the $\frac{3}{8}$ measure the three eighth notes are each counted as one beat. Therefore, the 1 and 2 of the $\frac{2}{4}$ measure is not the same speed as the 1, 2, 3 of the $\frac{3}{8}$ measure. Since the eighth notes are constant, the speed of the 1 an 2 an in $\frac{2}{4}$ equals the 1, 2, 3 of the $\frac{3}{8}$ measure.

40

Six Final Studies

I

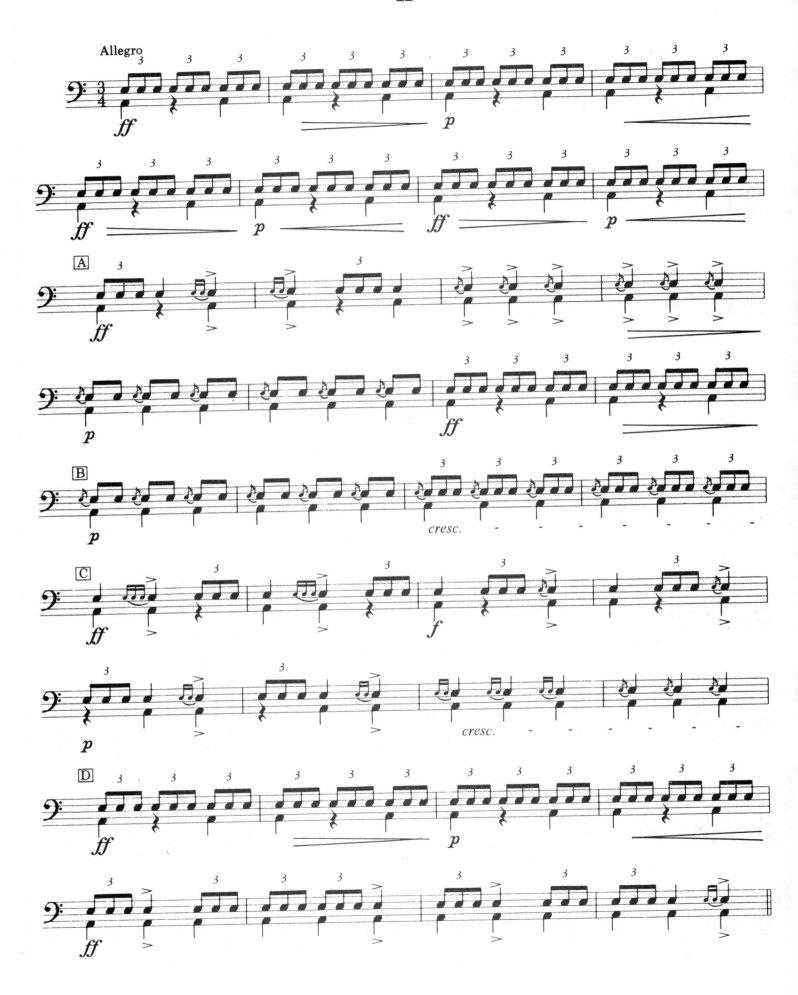

IV

VI

THE LOGIC OF IT ALL

BY ANTHONY J. CIRONE AND JOE SINAI

PROFESSIONAL
SECRETS
APPLYING
IMAGINATION TO
PERCUSSION
TECHNIQUES

Edited by Sondra Clark